S0-BJK-340

CHARACTERS AND KINGS

A Woman's Workshop
on the History of Israel

Books in this series—

CHARACTERS AND KINGS

A Woman's Workshop on the History of Israel

Part I

With Helps for Leaders

Carolyn Nystrom

G. Allen Fleece Library
Columbia International University
Columbia, SC 29203

Lamplighter
Books Grand Rapids,
Michigan
Zondervan Publishing House

Characters and Kings: A Woman's Workshop on the History of Israel Part 1

This is a Lamplighter Book
Published by the Zondervan Publishing House
1415 Lake Drive, S.E.
Grand Rapids, Michigan 49506

Copyright © 1985 by The Zondervan Corporation
Grand Rapids, Michigan

Library of Congress Cataloging in Publication Data
Nystrom, Carolyn.
    Characters and kings.
    (A Lamplighter book)
    Includes bibliographies and indexes.
    1. Bible. O.T. Kings—Outlines, syllabi, etc. 2. Jews—History—953–586
B.C.—Study and teaching. I. Title.
BS1335.5.N96 1985   222'.50076   84-27020
ISBN 0-310-41881-X (pt. 1)
ISBN 0-310-41871-2 (pt. 2)

Scripture taken from the *Holy Bible: New International Version*. Copyright 1978 by
the International Bible Society. Used by permission of Zondervan Bible Publishers.

The chart on pages 20–21 is reproduced from *A History of Israel* (Second Edition),
by John Bright. Copyright 1959 by W. L. Jenkins and 1972 by The Westminster
Press. Reproduced and used by permission.

All rights reserved. No part of this publication may be reproduced, stored in a
retrieval system, or transmitted in any form or by any means—electronic,
mechanical, photocopy, recording, or any other—except for brief quotations in
printed reviews, without the prior permission of the publisher.

Printed in the United States of America

85 86 87 88 89 90 / 10 9 8 7 6 5 4 3 2 1

CONTENTS

CHARACTERS AND KINGS

Four hundred years of Jewish history—that is the saga you are about to study. We pick up the narrative just after the death of the illustrious King David. The kingdom has expanded. Its influence throughout the region has reached its peak. The economy is stable. God-worship is firmly established. Patriotism is high. But David, a good king in spite of obvious shortcomings, is dead.

Enter Solomon—David's son and the first of twenty-two kings who will follow in David's genealogical line. These kings, along with scattered prophets, a host of kings from surrounding nations, and at least one vile queen, make up the characters of this narrative. It is no wonder that you'll need a chart to keep it all straight.

The complexities of the story will demand the reader's full attention, but the lively personalities of this era are worth the effort. You'll see Elijah, a fugitive prophet, hooting taunts at pagan worshipers while he humbly asks God to send fire from heaven to burn up his own small sacrifice. He got it.

You'll meet Jehu, who rides his chariot like a madman across the plains with a single bloodthirsty purpose in mind: to kill anyone connected with Ahab.

You'll know Josiah, the boy king, who turns his kingdom to God but can't persuade his own two sons, the future kings.

You'll visit Huldah, a woman prophet whom kings and priests consult when they need a direct word from God.

Four hundred years of Jewish history. Irrelevant today? Hardly. The apostle Paul, in his letter to the Christians at Rome, wrote of a giant tree with a grafted-in branch, that branch drawing strength from the deep root system of the ancient tree and bearing fruit for all to see. That grafted-in branch is the Christian church. Its root system? Judaism.

Thus, this ancient history of God's relationship to His chosen people becomes the history of all those grafted into a relationship with God through Jesus Christ. So Solomon and Elijah and Jehu and Huldah are not just amusing figures from a distant past. They are our history, our root system. We share their pain; we glory in their triumphs; and (if we are wise) we heed their warnings.

Immerse yourself in the characters and kings of Israel. You'll come out wiser.

Carolyn

I'VE JOINED THE GROUP. NOW WHAT?

You've joined a group of people who agree that the Bible is worth studying. For some it is the Word of God and therefore a standard for day-to-day decisions. Others may say the Bible is merely a collection of interesting teachings and tales, worthy of time and interest but not much more. You may place yourself at one end of this spectrum or the other. Or you may fit somewhere in between. But you have one goal in common with the other people in your group: to enjoy studying the Bible together.

In order for you to meet this goal, a few simple guidelines will prevent needless problems.

1. **Take a Bible with you.** Any modern translation is fine. Suggested versions include: Revised Standard Version, New American Standard Bible, Today's English Version, New International Version, Jerusalem Bible, New American Bible, and New English Bible.

A few versions, however, do not work well in group Bible

study. For beautiful language, the King James Version is unsurpassed. Yours may bear great sentimental value because it belonged to your grandmother. But if you use a King James Version, you will spend a great deal of effort translating the Elizabethan English into today's phrasing, perhaps losing valuable meaning in the process.

Paraphrases like Living Bible, Phillips, and Amplified are especially helpful in private devotions, but they lack the accuracy of a translation by Bible scholars. Therefore leave these at home on Bible-study day.

If you would like to match the phrasing of the questions in this guide, use the New International Version. If, however, you fear that any Bible is far too difficult for you to understand, try Today's English Version. This easy-to-read translation is certain to change your mind.

2. **Arrive at Bible study on time.** You'll feel as if you are half a step behind throughout the entire session if you miss the Bible readings and the opening survey questions.

3. **Come prepared.** A small section called "Preparing for Study" leads off each chapter. These studies form a bridge between each week's discussion. Don't stay home if you haven't done the work. But if you spend a few minutes during the week on the "Preparing for Study" assignments, you will greatly increase the value you receive from studying *Characters and Kings*. Use the space provided in your study guide to keep a record of your findings. You may need to refer to it during your group discussion.

Some people have trouble concentrating on a passage of Scripture if they read it for the first time during a group discussion. If you fall into that category, read it ahead of time while you are alone. But try to reserve final decisions about its meaning until you've had a chance to discuss it with the group.

4. **Use your chart.** Pages 20 and 21 should become the most well-worn pages of your study guide. Check them

sometime during each lesson to see how your current study fits into the larger picture of Israel and Judah under the kings.

5. **Call your hostess if you are going to be absent.** This saves her from setting a place for you if refreshments are served. It also frees the group to begin on time without waiting needlessly for you.

When you miss a session, study the passage independently. *Characters and Kings* forms a story. You'll feel more able to participate when you return if you have studied the intervening material.

6. **Volunteer to be a hostess.** A quick way to feel as if you belong is to have the Bible study meet at your house.

7. **Decide if you are a talker or a listener.** This is a discussion Bible study, and for a discussion to work well, all persons should participate more or less equally. If you are a talker, count to ten before you speak. Try waiting until several others speak before you give your own point of view.

If you are a listener, remind yourself that just as you benefit from what others say, they profit from your ideas. Besides, your insights will mean more even to you if you put them into words and say them out loud. So take courage and speak.

8. **Keep on track.** This is a group responsibility. Remember that you are studying the books of Kings and Chronicles. Although a speech, magazine article, or some other book may be related, discussion of it will take time away from the main object of your study. In the process, the whole group may go off into an interesting but time-consuming tangent, making the leader's job more difficult.

While the Bible is consistent within itself and many excellent topical studies build on its consistency, the purpose of this study is to examine thoroughly a four-hundred-year stretch of Israel's history. Therefore cross-referencing (comparing a passage with other portions of Scripture) will cause the same problems as any other tangent. In addition to confusing people who are unfamiliar with other parts of the Bible, cross-referencing may cause you to miss the writer's intent in the passage before you.

One unique feature of this study, however, is that Israel's history under the kings is covered in two, sometimes three, places in Scripture. These parallel passages are listed at the beginning of each study. Feel free to use them to shed light on your discussions. They are different views of the same event and come from the same source: God.

Naturally, once you have studied a section as a group, you may refer back to it. Each writer assumed his readers would have the earlier passages in mind as they read each new section.

9. **Help pace the study.** Each study should last about an hour and fifteen minutes. With the questions and your Bible in front of you, you can be aware of whether the study is progressing at an adequate pace. Each group member shares the responsibility of seeing that the entire passage is covered and that the study is brought to a profitable close.

10. **Don't criticize another church or religion.** You might find that the quiet person across the table attends that church—and she won't be back to your group.

11. **Get to know people in your group.** Call each other during the week between meetings. Meet socially; share a car pool when convenient; offer to take in a meal if another group member is ill. You may discover that you have more in common than a willingness to study the Bible. Perhaps you'll add to your list of friends.

12. **Get ready to lead.** It doesn't take a mature Bible student to lead this study. Just asking the questions in this guide should prompt a thorough digging into the passage. Besides, you'll find a hefty section of leaders' notes in the back in case you feel a little insecure. So once you've attended the group a few times, sign up to lead a discussion. Remember, the leader learns more than anyone else.

ME, A LEADER?

Sure. Many Bible-study groups share the responsibility of leading the discussion. Sooner or later your turn will come. Here are a few pointers to quell any rising panic and help you keep the group working together toward its common goal.

1. **Prepare well ahead of time.** A week or two in advance is not too much. Work through the "Preparing for Study" section, then read the Scripture discussion passage every day for several successive days. Go over the questions, writing out possible answers in your book. Check the leaders' helps at the back of the book for additional ideas, then read the questions again—several times—until the sequence and wording seem natural to you. Don't let yourself be caught during the study with that "now I wonder what comes next" feeling. Take careful note of the major areas of application. Try living them for a week. By then you will discover some of the difficulties others in your group will face when they try to

do the same. Finally, pray. Ask God to lead you as you lead the group. Ask Him to make you sensitive to people, to the Scripture, and to Himself. Expect to grow. You will.

2. **Pace the study.** Begin on time. People have come for the purpose of studying the Bible. You don't need to apologize for that. At the appointed hour, simply announce that it is time to begin, open with prayer, and launch into the study.

Keep an eye on the clock throughout the study. These questions are geared to last for about an hour and fifteen minutes. Don't spend forty-five minutes on the first three questions and then find you have to rush through the rest. On the other hand, if the questions are moving by too quickly, the group is probably not discussing each one thoroughly enough. Slow down. Encourage people to interact with each other's ideas. Be sure they are working through all aspects of the questions.

Then end—on time. Many people have other obligations immediately after the study and will appreciate a predictable closing time.

3. **Read the passage aloud by paragraphs—not verses.** Verse-by-verse reading causes a brief pause after each verse and breaks the flow of the narrative; this makes it harder to understand the total picture. So read by paragraphs.

4. **Use the chart and maps.** This study is a history. Time and place are important to each event. Refer to them sometime during each study so that your group continues to see each episode set in its larger story.

5. **Ask; don't tell.** This study guide is designed for a discussion moderated by a leader. It is not a teacher's guide. When you lead the group, your job is like that of a traffic director. You gauge the flow of discussion, being careful that everyone gets a turn. You decide which topics will be treated and in what order. You call a halt now and then to send

traffic in a new direction. But you do not mount a soapbox and lecture.

Your job is to help each person in the group to discover personally the meaning of the passage and to share that discovery with the others. Naturally, since you have prepared the lesson in advance, you will be tempted to tell them all you've learned. Resist this temptation until others have had a chance to discover the same things. Then, if something is still missing, you may add your own insight to the collection.

6. **Avoid tangents.** The bane of any discussion group is the oh-so-interesting lure of a tangent. These are always time consuming and rarely as profitable as the planned study. A few red flags will warn you that a tangent is about to arise. They are, "My pastor says . . ."; "I read that . . ."; "The other day Suzie . . ."; "If we look at Ezekiel (or John or Revelation) . . ."

If this occurs, politely listen to the first few sentences. If they confirm your suspicion that a tangent is indeed brewing, thank the person, then firmly but kindly direct attention back to the passage.

A leader does, however, need to be sensitive to pressing needs within a group. On rare occasions the tangent grows out of a need much more important than any preplanned study. In these cases, whisper a quick prayer for guidance and follow the tangent.

7. **Talk about application.** Each study in this guide leads to a discussion that applies the point of the passage to real life. If you are short of time or if your group feels hesitant about discussing personal things, you'll entertain the thought of omitting these questions. But if you do, your group will lose the main purpose of the study. If God's Word is a book to live by, a few people in your group ought to be willing to talk about how they are going to live in response to it. Putting

these intentions into words will strengthen their ability to live out the teachings. The listeners will be challenged to do the same.

So, always allow adequate time to talk over the application questions. Be prepared also to share from your own experience of trying to live out the passage.

8. **Try a prayer-'n'-share.** Many groups start their sessions with fifteen minutes of coffee, then hold a short time of sharing personal concerns, needs, and answers to prayer. Afterward, the group members pray briefly for each other, giving thanks and praise and asking together that God will meet the needs expressed. These short informal sentence prayers are much like casual sharing conversation. The group members simply turn their conversation away from each other and toward God. For many, this brief time of prayer becomes a weekly life line.

9. **Enjoy leading.** It's a big responsibility but a rewarding one.

BIBLE STUDY SCHEDULE

Date	Passage	Leader	Hostess
	1 Kings 3:1–28; 4:20–34		
	2 Chronicles 6–7		
	1 Kings 11		
	1 Kings 12		
	2 Chronicles 14–16		
	1 Kings 16:29–17:24		
	1 Kings 18		
	1 Kings 19		

Names and Phone Numbers

PLEASE CALL HOSTESS IF YOU CANNOT ATTEND

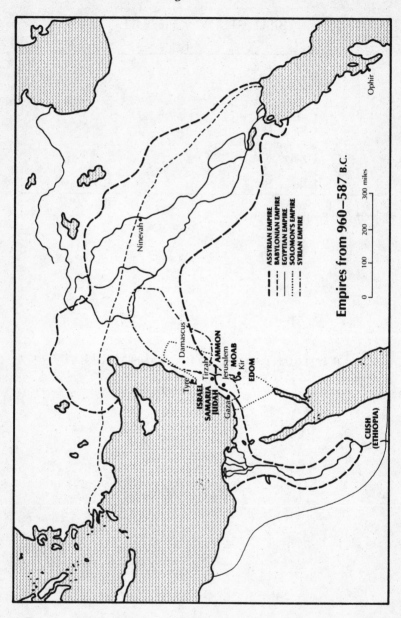

Empires from 960–587 B.C.

ASSYRIAN EMPIRE
BABYLONIAN EMPIRE
EGYPTIAN EMPIRE
SOLOMON'S EMPIRE
SYRIAN EMPIRE

0   100   200   300 miles

Ophir

Ninevah

Damascus

Tyre
ISRAEL
SAMARIA
JUDAH
Tirzah
Jerusalem
Gaza
AMMON
MOAB
Kir
EDOM

CUSH
(ETHIOPIA)

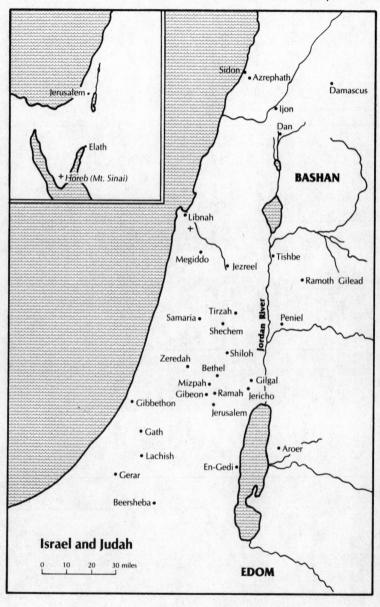

Jerusalem ●

Elath ●

+ Horeb (Mt. Sinai)

Sidon ●
● Azrephath
● Damascus

● Ijon

Dan ●

BASHAN

● Libnah
+

Megiddo ●
● Jezreel
● Tishbe
● Ramoth Gilead

Tirzah ●
Samaria ●
● Shechem
● Peniel

Zeredah ●
● Shiloh

● Bethel
Mizpah ●
● Gilgal
Gibeon ●
● Ramah
Jericho ●
Jerusalem ●

● Gibbethon

● Gath

● Lachish
● Aroer
En-Gedi ●

● Gerar

Beersheba ●

Jordan River

Israel and Judah

0   10   20   30 miles

EDOM

Date	EGYPT	JUDAH	ISRAEL	DAMASCUS	ASSYRIA
950		Solomon ca. 961–922		Rezon	Asshur-dan II 935–913
925	XXII Dynasty ca. 935–725 Shishak ca. 935–914	Rehoboam 922–915	Jeroboam I 922–901		
900	Osorkon I ca. 914–874	Abijah 915–913 Asa 913–873	Nadab 901–900 Baasha 900–877		Adad-nirari II 912–892
875			Elah 877–876 Zimri 876	Ben-hadad I ca. 885–870	Asshur-nasir-pal II 884–860
		Jehoshaphat 873–849	Omri 876–869 Ahab 869–850 (Elijah) (Battle of Qarqar 853)	Ben-hadad II ca. 870–842	
850		Jehoram 849–843 Ahaziah 843/2 Athaliah 842–837 Joash 837–800	Ahaziah 850–849 Jehoram (Elisha) 849–843/2 Jehu 843/2–815		Shalmaneser III 859–825
825				Hazael ca. 842–806	Shamshi-adad V 824–812
800		Amaziah 800–783	Jehoahaz 815–802 Jehoash 802–786	Ben-hadad III	Adad-nirari III 811–784
775	XXIII Dynasty ca. 759–715	Uzziah (Azariah) 783–742	Jeroboam II 786–746		Assyrian weakness
750			(Amos)		

Schism to Mid-Eighth Century

	EGYPT	JUDAH	ISRAEL	DAMASCUS	ASSYRIA
					Assyrian weakness
775	XXII Dynasty ca. 935–725	Uzziah 783–742	Jeroboam II 786–746		
	XXIII Dynasty ca. 759–715	(Jotham coregent ca. 750) Jotham 742–735			Tiglath-pileser III 745–727
750		(Isaiah) (Micah)	(Amos) (Hosea)	Rezin ca. 740–732	
			Zechariah 746–745		
			Shallum 745		
			Menahem 745–737		
			Pekahiah 737–736		
	XXIV Dynasty ca. 725–709	Ahaz 735–715	Pekah 736–732		Shalmaneser V 726–722
725			Hoshea 732–724		Sargon II 721–705
	XXV (Ethiopian) Dyn. ca. 716/15–663	Hezekiah 715–687/6	Fall of Samaria 722/1		
	Shabako ca. 710/9–696/5 (?)	701 Sennacherib	invades		Sennacherib 704–681
700	Shebteko ca. 696/5–685/4 (?)	688 ? Sennacherib	invades ?		Esarhaddon 680–669
	(Tirhakah coregent ca. 690/89) (?)	Manasseh 687/6–642			
	Tirhakah ca. (690) 685/4–664				
675	Invasions of	Egypt: Sack of Thebes 663			Asshurbanapal 668–627
	XXVI Dynasty 664–525	Amon 642–640		Medes	
650	Psammetichus I 664–610	Josiah 640–609			
		(Zephaniah) (Jeremiah)	Neo-Babylonian Empire		
625		(Nahum)	Nabopolassar 626–605	Cyaxares ca. 625–585	Sin-shar-ishkun 629–612
	Neco II 610–594	Jehoahaz 609			Fall of Nineveh 612
		Jehoiakim 609–598	Nebuchadnezzar 605/4–562		Asshur-uballit II 612–609
600	Psammetichus II 594–589	(Habakkuk)			
		Jehoiachin 598/7			
		Zedekiah 597–587 (Ezekiel)		Astyages 585–550	
575	Apries (Hophra) 589–570	Fall of Jerusalem 587 Exile			

Schism to Mid-Eighth Century

Note: There may be slight variances in dates and spellings of names with the NIV, but none of these seriously affects the overall picture.

1

PREPARING FOR STUDY

Proverbs 27; Ecclesiastes 3:1–14; Proverbs 17; Psalm 127; Song of Songs 8:5–7

Solomon wrote thousands of songs and proverbs. The following may have been among his writings. Spread your reading of these over several days. As you read each one, ask yourself the following questions and write your answers on a separate sheet of paper:

1. What kind of person would have written this?

2. What universal truths are portrayed here?

3. When have I experienced one of these truths?

Passage	Question 1	Question 2	Question 3
Proverbs 27			
Ecclesiastes 3:1–14			
Proverbs 17			
Psalm 127			
Song of Songs 8:5–7			

4. Read "I've Joined the Group. Now What?" and "Me, a Leader?" (pp. 9–16) to form a common basis for group study.

1

SOLOMON: PRAYING WITH GOD'S VALUES

1 Kings 3:1–28; 4:20–34*

My hand trembled as I dialed the phone. I hesitated, put down the receiver, then dialed again. Finally I heard a businesslike *hello* on the other end.

"Hello, Mary? I need a listening ear. Do you have time?" Haltingly I poured out my disappointment and sorrow about a problem that had been plaguing me for days. Mary made sympathetic noises, offered a few corrective comments, and promised to pray. The situation was unchanged; yet as the day progressed, I felt the cloud of sadness lift. I knew Mary was praying. And God, in His generosity, was granting the requests of her prayer.

But why had I chosen Mary to share my grief? Because she was approachable? Partly. But more because I knew her spiritual walk; it was carefully metered by God's laws. And

*Parallel passage, 2 Chronicles 1

because I had often heard her pray. She was comfortable with prayer; her prayers were specific and to the point. Like her walk, her prayers seemed closely matched to God's values. I felt sure that God would hear and answer her.

King Solomon was no spiritual giant. But on at least one occasion he prayed for exactly what God had in mind to give.

1. If God were to appear to you and say, "Name one thing you want; you may have it," what would you ask for? ＿

＿＿＿＿＿＿＿＿＿＿＿＿＿＿＿＿＿＿＿＿＿＿

If God were to appear in this way to your national leader, what would you want him or her to ask for? ＿＿

＿＿＿＿＿＿＿＿＿＿＿＿＿＿＿＿＿＿＿＿＿＿

＿＿＿＿＿＿＿＿＿＿＿＿＿＿＿＿＿＿＿＿＿＿

Read aloud 1 Kings 3:1–9.

2. a. What were some of Solomon's actions in the early years of his reign? ＿＿＿＿＿＿＿＿＿＿＿＿＿

＿＿＿＿＿＿＿＿＿＿＿＿＿＿＿＿＿＿＿＿＿＿

＿＿＿＿＿＿＿＿＿＿＿＿＿＿＿＿＿＿＿＿＿＿

＿＿＿＿＿＿＿＿＿＿＿＿＿＿＿＿＿＿＿＿＿＿

＿＿＿＿＿＿＿＿＿＿＿＿＿＿＿＿＿＿＿＿＿＿

b. What do these actions say about Solomon's character?

＿＿＿＿＿＿＿＿＿＿＿＿＿＿＿＿＿＿＿＿＿＿

＿＿＿＿＿＿＿＿＿＿＿＿＿＿＿＿＿＿＿＿＿＿

＿＿＿＿＿＿＿＿＿＿＿＿＿＿＿＿＿＿＿＿＿＿

3. Read Deuteronomy 12:1–7. What problems do you anticipate will result from Solomon's failure to obey this command from God? ＿＿＿＿＿＿＿＿＿＿＿＿＿

_____

_____

4. Look again at 1 Kings 3:5—9. What connections does Solomon see between himself and his father David?

_____

5. What does Solomon's response to God's question suggest about his attitude toward himself, his job, and his God? (Use all of verses 5—9.) _____

_____

_____

_____

_____

Read aloud 1 Kings 3:10—15.

6. a. What did God promise Solomon? _____

_____

_____

_____

_____

b. What was to be the extent of these gifts? _____

_____

_____

c. What conditions did God attach to granting Solomon long life? _____

_____

d. What change did these promises bring in Solomon's behavior? _____

_____

7. How would you describe a discerning heart? _____

_____

_____

_____

8. Why was Solomon's prayer for a discerning heart likely to please God? _____

_____

_____

9. Think of one person who particularly needs a discerning heart right now. Pray one or two sentences asking God's help for that person. _____

_____

Read aloud 1 Kings 3:16–28.

10. Imagine yourself as a bystander in King Solomon's court. What emotions would you feel during the different stages of the hearing? _____

_____

_____

_____

11. a. Do you agree that Solomon's method of judgment was wise? Why, or why not? (Consider the other possible outcomes.) _____

_____

_____

_____

b. How did the child stand to benefit from this decision?

_____

_____

Read aloud 1 Kings 4:20–34.

12. In what specific ways did God answer Solomon's prayer of 1 Kings 3:7–9? _____

_____

_____

_____

_____

13. As you compare Solomon's prayer with God's response, what conclusions can you draw about God's values? ____

_____

_____

14. What benefits might a church or a family reap because one of its members knows how to pray within God's will? _____

_____

_____

_____

_____

15. When your own prayers do not seem to coincide with the will of God, what is the most likely cause of the problem? _____

_____

_____

16. How can you begin to bring your prayers more into line
    with God's values? _____

    _____

    _____

    _____

2

PREPARING FOR STUDY

2 Chronicles 2–5*

Read all of 2 Chronicles 2–5.

1. a. What purpose did Solomon see for God's temple (2:3–6)?

   b. What could that temple not do?

2. What does the communication between King Solomon and King Hiram suggest that they believed to be true about God?

3. Notice the details describing God's temple. Why do you think Solomon built such an elaborate temple with such care?

4. In what different ways did the people of Israel express their worship when they brought the ark of God to the new temple?

Read 1 Kings 6:11–13.

5. What was more important to God than a beautiful building?

6. Make a quick mental survey of your lifestyle as it compares with what you know of God's laws. Do you

---

*Parallel passage, 1 Kings 5:1–8:21

behave in any ways that might be forming a barrier between you and God?

If you are able to, talk to God about this.

7. Have you read "I've Joined the Group. Now What?" and "Me, a Leader?" (pp. 9–16) yet? If not, do so this week.

2

SOLOMON: BEARING GOD'S NAME

2 Chronicles 6–7*

"I now pronounce you husband and wife. What God has joined, let no man put asunder."

With these traditional words, a wedding ends. Two people who entered the church separately, leave united as one. They even carry the same last name. And after that point anything that one or the other does will reflect on that name. Reasonable or not, the reputation of each person will rise and fall with the partner's behavior. It's enough to give a newly engaged couple some very solemn thoughts.

But God Himself takes the same risk—and not with just one person, but with a whole group. God calls them "my people who are called by my Name." What a great privilege to be linked to the name of God. And what a heavy responsibility.

---

*Parallel passage, 1 Kings 8:22–9:9

Read aloud 2 Chronicles 6:1–11.

1. What qualities of God are revealed in Solomon's account of Jewish history? _____

_____

_____

2. Find as many repetitions as you can of the phrase "for my Name." What does this phrase emphasize about the function of the temple? _____

_____

_____

Read aloud 2 Chronicles 6:12–21.

3. What did Solomon express by the position of his body during his prayer? _____

_____

_____

4. a. Notice the words *covenant* and *promise* in verses 14–17. What had God promised Israel? _____

_____

_____

   b. What conditions were attached to that promise? _____

_____

_____

5. How does Solomon answer his own question of verse 18: "But will God really dwell on earth with men?" (What does he ask of God? What does he not expect?)

_____

_____

_____

6. If this chapter accurately describes God's nature, why might you need and want His forgiveness? _____

_____

_____

Read aloud by paragraphs 2 Chronicles 6:22–42.

7. For each paragraph answer the following questions (not every paragraph will have an answer for each question):

a. What situation does Solomon describe?

b. What does Solomon ask God to do?

c. What reasons does Solomon give God for granting that request?

Verses	a	b	c
22–23			
24–25			
26–27			
28–31			
32–33			
34–35			
36–39			
40–42			

8. As you compare verses 14–16 with Solomon's requests to God, what does he seem to understand about his people and their future? _____

_____

_____

Read aloud 2 Chronicles 7:1–10.

9. a. In what ways did the people express their worship of
God? _____

_____

_____

_____

b. What do you think God meant by His response to
Solomon's prayer? _____

_____

_____

Read aloud 2 Chronicles 7:11–22.

10. In what ways does God connect Solomon with His
people? _____

_____

11. a. What did it mean for Israel to be called by the name of
God? _____

_____

b. What responsibilities did this bring? _____

_____

_____

c. What blessings? _____

_____

_____

d. What warnings? _____

_____

_____

12. According to these verses, why would God turn away from His people? _____

_____

_____

13. a. What steps could the people take to restore their relationship with God? _____

_____

_____

b. What ingredients would make up that restoration? ___

_____

_____

14. a. Prayerfully read again verse 14. Think of a group of people whose relationship with God needs restoring (your family, your church, your community, your nation). _____

b. How could you, as a part of that group, begin to contribute to a restored relationship with God? _____

_____

_____

c. Pray aloud briefly for this group you have chosen.

3

PREPARING FOR STUDY

2 Chronicles 8:1–9:28*

Read 2 Chronicles 8.

1. Find fifteen accomplishments of Solomon's reign.

2. In light of these accomplishments, what would the people of Israel expect in the future? Read 2 Chronicles 9:1–28. Take note of each indication of opulence.

3. If you visited such a kingdom, what would impress you?

4. Verse 23 describes Solomon's wisdom as "the wisdom God had put in his heart." What comments in this chapter express the magnitude of this gift from God?

5. As you look back through these two chapters, what reasons did the people of Israel have for believing that their king was pleasing God? Review Deuteronomy 12:1–7. Now look at 2 Chronicles 8:11.

6. What hint do you find of Solomon's beliefs about God?

7. When have your own actions betrayed an attempt to separate spiritual living from everyday living?

8. What harmful effect might these actions have on you and those close to you?

Talk to God about it.

*Parallel passage, 1 Kings 9:10–10:29

3

SOLOMON: FAITHLESS IN LOVE

*1 Kings 11**

"Help me decide what to do, pastor." The young woman sat across the desk from her minister. "I want to do God's will if only I knew what it was." She spoke with cheerful confidence. "God has brought Bill and me together, and He has created a great love between us. Bill wants to marry me, but I'm not sure."

"But has Bill given himself to Jesus Christ?" her pastor probed.

"No, not yet," she hesitated. "But I think he will—perhaps after we're married . . ." Her voice trailed off under her pastor's firm gaze.

"God has already shown you His will, I think," her pastor replied. "You know Paul's writings to the Christians at Corinth: 'Do not be yoked together with unbelievers.' "

*Parallel passage, 2 Chronicles 9:29–31

The woman nodded reluctantly.

God's rules for living may seem harsh, especially to someone in the situation described here. But these laws are often less harsh than the results of living by our own guidelines. God seems to know what works. Solomon had occasion to discover this truth.

Read aloud 1 Kings 11:1–13.

1. What negative effects did wealth and power have on Solomon? _____

   _____

   _____

   _____

   _____

2. Why had God commanded His people not to intermarry with the nations around them? _____

   _____

   _____

3. In what ways did Solomon break the first commandment: "Thou shalt have no other gods before me"? _____

   _____

   _____

4. a. What punishment would come to Solomon because of this sin? _____

   _____

b. What mercy does God promise? _____

_____

_____

c. Why? _____

_____

5. Why do you think God views idolatry so sternly? _____

_____

_____

Read aloud 1 Kings 11:14–25.

6. Notice the repeated phrase, "The LORD raised up against Solomon an adversary." What mixture of spiritual and political forces does this suggest? _____

_____

_____

7. What indications do you see that these two men had the potential to become serious threats to Solomon? (Treat Hadad and Rezon separately.) _____

_____

_____

_____

_____

Read aloud 1 Kings 11:26–40.

8. How did God use Ahijah's new cloak as a message to Jeroboam? _____

_____

_____

9. a. What reasons did the prophet give for God's promised
action against Solomon? _____

_____

_____

b. What did He promise Jeroboam? _____

_____

_____

c. What conditions did He attach to those promises? ____

_____

d. What limitations did God put on His punishment of
Solomon? _____

_____

_____

10. If Jeroboam chose to benefit from the experience of
Israel's previous two kings, how would it affect his reign?

_____

_____

_____

_____

11. Verse 9 says that God had twice appeared personally to
Solomon. (Review briefly 1 Kings 3:4–15 and 9:1–9.)
How might Solomon have drawn on these two encoun-
ters with God to prevent the problems he now faced? ____

_____

_____

_____

Read aloud 1 Kings 11:41–43.

12. As you look back at Solomon's life, what do you find to admire? _____

_____

_____

13. Verse 6 characterizes Solomon's life with the words, "So Solomon did evil in the eyes of the LORD." Why do you think God described such a successful king in this way?

_____

_____

14. If you were to name one sin that brought this description on Solomon, what would it be? _____

_____

15. Solomon's marriages to pagans testified to his lack of wholehearted commitment to God. If God were to point out a soft area in your own life, where your actions do not live up to your supposed beliefs, what area would it be? _____

_____

_____

4

PREPARING FOR STUDY

1 Kings 13–14*

Immediately after Solomon's death, civil war erupted in Israel. Jeroboam became king of the North, and Rehoboam, Solomon's son, became king of the South (Judah). This week's reading draws three vignettes of life during that civil war.

Read 1 Kings 13.

1. What was hard about the job God gave to the man that He sent from Judah to the North?

2. In what ways did God show His power through this man?

3. In what sense was the old prophet of verse 11 a false messenger?

4. How did the old prophet's encounter with a genuine man of God enable him to become a true prophet? (What words and actions show this change?)

Read 1 Kings 14:1–20. Review also God's promise to Jeroboam in 1 Kings 11:37–39.

5. What results can you see of Jeroboam's failure to obey God (results that affect Jeroboam, his family, his people)?

*Parallel passage, 2 Chronicles 12

Read 1 Kings 14:21–31.

6. The scene now changes to Judah, the southern kingdom. What evidence do you find there of spiritual ill-health?

7. Notice Rehoboam's makeshift bronze shields. What fake spiritual values do these remind you of in your own life?

4

JEROBOAM/REHOBOAM: CIVIL WAR

*1 Kings 12**

Civil war. Our American minds turn to Yankee blue battling Confederate gray; brothers, cousins, and neighbors pitted against each other; a wantonly destructive march to the sea—forever an embarrassment to both sides; a president on his knees, in tears.

Three thousand years ago, Israel, too, suffered civil war with many of the same griefs. As in our own war, family members had to decide which side they were on. Geography wasn't always the most important factor, for this war was not only a war of politics; it was also, at least at the outset, a war of faith.

---

*Parallel passage, 2 Chronicles 10–11

Read aloud 1 Kings 12:1–24.

1. What steps in this chapter led to the division recorded in verse 20? _____

_____

_____

_____

_____

2. a. At what points did reconciliation seem possible? _____

_____

_____

   b. What volatile words and actions on both sides fanned the disagreement into open war? _____

_____

_____

_____

3. What indications do you find that God had not abandoned His people during this time of conflict? _____

_____

_____

_____

4. If you had to go through a civil war, of what value would it be for you to know that God is always in control? _____

_____

_____

Read aloud 1 Kings 12:25–33.

5. a. Find on your maps (pp. 18–19) the places mentioned in these verses. _____

_____

   b. What geographic reasons can you see for Jeroboam's selection of these sites? _____

_____

_____

_____

6. What motivated Jeroboam to set up alternate places of worship? _____

_____

_____

_____

7. Read God's law to the Jewish people in Deuteronomy 12:5–7. Now read again 1 Kings 12:28–30. What spiritual results for the people of Israel would you expect to grow out of Jeroboam's new places of worship? _____

_____

_____

Note: These two places of false worship (Bethel and Dan) appear again and again throughout the next two hundred years of Jewish history. Keep an eye open for them as you study *Characters and Kings* and as you do any supplementary reading in the Prophets. They eventually become the partial cause for the separation of the Jews of Judah and a people later called the *Samaritans*.

8. Focus on verses 31–33. What other things did Jeroboam do that were contrary to God's law for His people? (Find all that you can.) _____

_____

_____

_____

_____

9. a. If you had been a godly person living under Jeroboam's rule, what choices would you have had to make? _____

_____

_____

_____

b. What would be hard about those choices? _____

_____

_____

_____

Read aloud 2 Chronicles 11:5, 11–17.

10. a. How did the people described here solve the problem of divided loyalties? _____

_____

_____

_____

b. What effect would their decision have on the two countries? _____

_____

_____

11. a. Suppose you were placed in a setting as hostile to your faith as Israel under Jeroboam. What would you miss most? _____

_____

_____

_____

  b. What steps would you take to preserve your faith? ____

_____

_____

_____

12. a. In what ways do your actions show a take-it-for-granted attitude toward your current opportunities to worship? _____

_____

_____

  b. What steps could you take to worship God more fully?

_____

_____

_____

_____

5

PREPARING FOR STUDY

2 Chronicles 13*

Read 2 Chronicles 11:18–23 as background for Abijah's reign. Then read 2 Chronicles 13.

1. What reasons did Abijah have to respect Jeroboam's army?

2. Look again at Abijah's speech in verses 4–12. What contrasts did Abijah draw between his kingdom and Jeroboam's?

3. How much of Abijah's speech do you think was political strutting, and how much was honest warning?

4. As you think through this chapter, what reasons can you see for Abijah's successful reign?

5. Notice the way Jeroboam's life ended in verses 19–20. Then review God's promises to Jeroboam in 1 Kings 11:37–39. After such an optimistic beginning, why do you think his life ended in this way?

6. What effect do you think your own spiritual development is having on the total course of your life?

*Parallel passage, 1 Kings 15:1–8

5

ASA: SEEKER OF GOD

2 Chronicles 14–16*

My friend Susan, emotionally raw from a recent divorce, attended a Fourth of July picnic with some friends, only to discover that the one thing more lonely than being alone is being alone in a crowd. She came home feeling not only husbandless, but feeling that her life was without God. For twenty years she had willed God out of existence. Now, more alone than ever, she stretched out on her empty bed and spoke the hesitant beginnings of a prayer, "God, if You are there . . ."

So began a tortuous journey toward faith—a seeking after God. And God heard her prayer; bit by bit, God Almighty revealed Himself to Susan.

*Parallel passage, 1 Kings 15:9–24

Read aloud 2 Chronicles 14.

1. a. List the action words in verses 1–7. _____

_____

_____

_____

_____

   b. What do these action words tell you about Asa? _____

_____

_____

_____

2. What does Asa's prayer (verse 11) reveal about his relationship with God? _____

_____

_____

3. a. According to Asa's actions and his prayer, what did he believe to be true about God? _____

_____

_____

_____

_____

_____

   b. What events recorded in this chapter suggest that Asa's beliefs were correct? _____

_____

_____

_____

Read aloud 2 Chronicles 15.

4. Focus on God's message to Asa in verses 1–7. What past conditions in Israel might cause Asa to listen carefully to God's message? _____

_____

_____

_____

_____

5. What warnings and blessings are implied in Azariah's prophecy? _____

_____

_____

6. a. Look again at verses 8–19. What words and phrases show the wholeheartedness with which Asa and his people turned to God? _____

_____

_____

_____

_____

_____

b. What changes can you imagine in the day-to-day living of ordinary people because of this reform? _____

_____

_____

Note: "Canaanite religion presents us with no pretty picture. . . . Female deities included Asherah. . . . These Goddesses, though fluid in personality and function, represented the female principal in the fertility cult. They are portrayed as sacred courtesans or pregnant mothers or, with a surprising polarity, as blood thirsty goddesses of war. . . . As in all such religions, numerous debasing practices, including sacred prostitution, homosexuality and various orgiastic rites, were prevalent. It was the sort of religion with which Israel, however much she might borrow from the culture of Canaan, could never with good conscience make peace" (Bright, pp. 118–19).

7. a. Review God's law to His people regarding idolatry found in Deuteronomy 17:2–7. What safeguards against injustice did this law provide? _____

_____

_____

_____

   b. In view of Judah's current setting, how might this law be an asset? (Consider spiritual, political, moral, emotional aspects.) _____

_____

_____

_____

Read aloud 2 Chronicles 16.

8. a. In what ways do Asa's actions near the end of his life not live up to his previous ideals? _____

_____

_____

_____

b. As you read of the last events in Asa's life, what
emotions do you feel? Why? _____

_____

_____

9. a. Note the people and places mentioned in verses 1–6.
(Locate these on the chart and maps on pp. 18–21.) ___

_____

b. What spiritual and political implications to Asa's treaty
with Ben-Hadad do you see? _____

_____

_____

_____

10. a. Read again the prophecy of Hanani in verses 7–9.
How is this message from God different from the
previous prophecy? (See 15:1–7.) _____

_____

_____

_____

b. As you study these two prophecies, what does God
seem to expect of His followers? _____

_____

_____

11. Notice the repeated idea: If you seek the Lord, He will
be found by you. What does this suggest about the

nature of spiritual development? _____

_____

_____

_____

12. At your current stage of spiritual development, what steps could you take right now to seek the Lord? _____

_____

_____

_____

6

PREPARING FOR STUDY

1 Kings 15:25–16:34*

While Asa was ruling in Judah, many changes were taking place in the northern kingdom of Israel.

Read of these in 1 Kings 15:25–16:34.

1. Clarify the events in your mind by filling in the chart below.

Name	Length of reign	Significant incidents	Good or evil?	Why?	Role of prophet	Manner of death
Nadab						
Baasha						
Elah						
Zimri						
Omri						
Ahab						

2. Now look at how this fits into the larger framework of history by studying the chart on pages 20–21.

---

*Parallel passage, 2 Chronicles 16.

3. Notice the repeated description: These kings walked in the ways of Jeroboam. What do these words suggest about the responsibility of this first leader of the North?

4. If God were to call a powerful prophet to minister to the northern kingdom now, what points of conflict would you expect?

6

ELIJAH: BUILDING TRUST

1 Kings 16:29—17:24

I once watched a young father and his friend use his year-old child as a "ball" for a game of catch. The men stood about six feet apart. One gently swung the child behind him and arched him carefully in the air. The other matched the arc with his arms and caught him so smoothly that the boy hardly knew he was no longer airborne. A few grandmotherly types standing nearby eyed the concrete floor, paled, and clutched their hearts. But the boy giggled delightedly with each new swoop. He trusted his daddy.

That trust had not sprouted full-grown overnight. His dad had played "horsy" with him on his knee, had ridden him high on his shoulders, had taught him to walk. No mishaps then; no mishaps now.

God teaches trust in much the same way—to Elijah and to us.

Read aloud 1 Kings 16:29–34.

1. What words and phrases help you understand the spiritual climate in Israel during Ahab's reign? _____

_____

_____

_____

_____

_____

2. What kinds of things would have to happen for the people of Israel to know God? _____

_____

_____

_____

_____

Read aloud 1 Kings 17:1.

3. What can you know of Elijah from this verse? (Find all that you can.) _____

_____

_____

_____

4. If God caused this prophecy to be fulfilled, what would you expect to happen to the people? _____

_____

_____

to King Ahab? _____

_____

to Elijah? _____

_____

Read aloud 1 Kings 17:2–16.

5. a. Imagine yourself in the situation described in verses
    2–7. What would have been difficult about Elijah's
    stay at Kerith? _____

    _____

    _____

    _____

    _____

   b. If Elijah used this time to learn from God, what truths
    do you think would have been impressed on him? ____

    _____

    _____

6. Look again at verses 7–16. What details show the
   severity of the drought? _____

   _____

   _____

   _____

7. Why might the widow have considered Elijah's requests
   presumptuous? _____

   _____

   _____

8. What could the widow have learned about God because of Elijah's stay with her? _____

_____

_____

_____

Read aloud 1 Kings 17:17–24.

9. Notice the questions in these verses. What do they suggest about the relationships among the widow and Elijah and God? _____

_____

_____

_____

10. What lasting effects would this miracle have on the boy? The widow? Elijah? _____

_____

_____

_____

_____

11. Scan the whole chapter. What demonstrations of supernatural power do you find? _____

_____

_____

_____

12. How might each of these events have helped Elijah to trust God? _____

_____

_____

_____

13. As you look back at your own walk with God, what events has God used to help you trust Him? _____

_____

_____

_____

14. In what ways can you draw on the trust God has built in the past as you perform your current responsibilities? ____

_____

_____

_____

7

PREPARING FOR STUDY

Luke 1:1–25

Get ready for this week's study by reading a New Testament passage that looks back at Elijah and looks forward to Christ.

Read Luke 1:1–25.

1. What credentials for writing does Luke credit to himself?

2. What can you know about Elizabeth and Zechariah from these verses?

3. Concentrate on verses 13–17. What does the angel Gabriel predict about this baby? (John was later known as John the Baptist.)

4. Notice the response of the prospective parents. What does this response reveal about the importance they placed on the angel's message?

5. Look again at verse 17. In what ways was the spirit and power of Elijah to be displayed in John?

6. What do you know about Elijah that suggests characteristics similar to what the angel describes?

7. Why might God call similar prophets in the time of Ahab and in the time just prior to Christ's coming?

7

ELIJAH: MIRROR OF GOD'S POWER

1 Kings 18

What is the power of almighty God? This is the God who flung out a universe—made from nothing. He created water and land and lightning and the tiniest microorganism and the intricacies of the human body.

How did God create? What were His methods? What was time before there was time? These are God's secrets. We only know that God spoke. And it happened. The rest is veiled.

Occasionally in history, God draws aside that veil and lets us see, for a moment, an image of His power. Miracles occur. Our minds, regimented by reliable laws of nature, rebel against these intrusions upon predictability. We forget, momentarily, that the God who made nature's laws also controls them.

Elijah lived at such a time. And God used Elijah as a mirror of His power.

Read aloud 1 Kings 18:1–19.

1. If you had been Elijah hearing God's command of verse 1, what thoughts would have gone through your mind?

   _____

2. What indications do you find of the severity of the drought? _____

   _____

   _____

3. What can you know of the spiritual conditions in Israel?

   _____

   _____

4. Notice the difference in the way Obadiah and Ahab greeted Elijah. What contrast does this illustrate in their characters? _____

   _____

   _____

5. Look through these verses again noticing particularly Obadiah. In what ways did Obadiah acknowledge God's authority? _____

   _____

   _____

Read aloud 1 Kings 18:20–39.

6. What details make this story come alive in your mind?

   _____

   _____

_____

_____

7. a. Notice Elijah's challenge in verse 21. What does it imply about religion in Israel? _____

_____

_____

b. How might an Israelite, who was attempting to be broad-minded, defend this kind of wavering? _____

_____

_____

_____

8. What effects have you experienced when you waver over the issue of who (or what) is god of your life? _____

_____

_____

_____

9. Why is this kind of wavering harmful? _____

_____

_____

_____

10. What was at stake in this confrontation? (Draw from all you have read so far.) _____

_____

_____

_____

_____

11. How did Elijah, in his preparation, add importance to this confrontation? _____

_____

_____

_____

_____

12. Study Elijah's prayer. What did Elijah ask God to do? _____

_____

_____

13. To what extent did God answer Elijah's prayer? _____

_____

Read aloud 1 Kings 18:40–46.

14. What evidences do you find here of Elijah's faith? _____

_____

_____

_____

15. Put yourself in Ahab's place as his chariot raced down the mountain. What would you see, hear, feel? _____

_____

_____

16. Scan the entire chapter. In what ways do you see the power of God demonstrated through Elijah? _____

_____

_____

_____

17. Look again at the wavering described in verse 21. How
    might the power of God displayed in this chapter help
    you deal with your own temptations to waver? _____

_____

_____

_____

8

PREPARING FOR STUDY

James 5:13–20

Read James 5:13–20.

1. Circle the words *pray, prayer, prayed* in this text. According to these verses, in what different circumstances is it appropriate to pray?

2. What parts do believers, as a group, have in these kinds of prayers?

3. What would be lost if a Christian always had to pray alone?

4. What could a modern-day believer learn about prayer from Elijah?

5. a. Suppose that you were placed in an environment where you were the only person who worshiped the true God. What difficulties would this present?

   b. What would you hope God would do for you?

8

ELIJAH: A PROPHET DEPRESSED

1 Kings 19

A Christian writer sat alone in her dark basement, covered her head with her arms, and cried, "God, why won't You just let me die?"

A Christian mother and energetic leader in her church found her mind so engulfed by thoughts of suicide that she fled, quite sensibly, to a psychologist.

A Christian youth worker hooked a hose to his car exhaust pipe and . . . (he was found in time).

God's people are not immune to depression—and neither was the great prophet Elijah.

Read aloud 1 Kings 19:1–9a.

1. a. What was the personal cost to Elijah of his spiritual triumph in the previous chapter? _____

_____

_____

_____

_____

b. What had Jezebel failed to learn from the events on Mount Carmel? _____

_____

_____

2. Notice the times and distances in this account. What do these tell you about the scope of Elijah's problem? _____

_____

_____

_____

3. In what ways did God's help seem to match Elijah's needs? _____

_____

_____

_____

Read aloud 1 Kings 19:9b–14.

4. If you had stood in the mouth of the cave beside Elijah, what effect would these events have had on you? _____

_____

_____

5. a. In view of Elijah's personality and circumstances, why do you think God showed him the wind, the earthquake, and the fire? _____

_____

_____

_____

_____

b. Why do you think God chose to appear in the still, small voice? _____

_____

_____

6. a. Notice God's questions and Elijah's answers (verses 9b–10 and 13b–14). What reasons did Elijah have for wanting to die? _____

_____

_____

b. What does this repetition suggest about the intensity of Elijah's despair? _____

_____

_____

Read aloud 1 Kings 19:15–21.

7. What further steps did God take to relieve Elijah's depression? _____

_____

_____

_____

Note: *New Bible Commentary* says the word *anoint* implies a call for a special purpose, whether or not there is an actual ceremony of anointing.

8. What mixed feelings do you think these words from God prompted in Elijah? _____

_____

_____

9. What do Elisha's actions suggest about his response to this new calling? _____

_____

_____

_____

10. a. Survey briefly all of chapter 19. What evidence do you find that Elijah was seriously discouraged? _____

_____

_____

_____

_____

_____

b. Look again at everything Elijah says to God. What does this suggest as one appropriate way for God's people to deal with depression? _____

_____

_____

11. a. In what different ways did God support Elijah during this difficult time? _____

_____

_____

_____

_____

_____

_____

b. As you review each of God's actions, what kinds of
help do you think a follower of God can expect from
Him during a time of discouragement? _____

_____

_____

_____

_____

12. As you deal with your own current discouragements,
what kind of help do you need from God? _____

_____

_____

_____

_____

13. Elijah prayed for death, but God gave him an assistant
instead. What does this suggest about God's possible
solutions to your own particular discouragements? _____

_____

_____

_____

HEY, THIS STORY'S NOT FINISHED!

Is Elijah off the hook forever now that he has an assistant? Or is he going to flutter back into the narrative whenever God needs a big gun? And what about Ahab and Jezebel? Do they get off free after defying God and massacring His people?

And Solomon. Is all of the influence he wielded gone to nothing? Or will his line of kings forever feel the effect of Solomon and his father David? If so, will that line of kings follow the good or the bad example of their ancestors?

You are right; the story is not finished. *Characters and Kings* has a Part 2. It begins where this story leaves off—with Jezebel. In Part 2, you'll get an intimate picture of what makes this angry queen storm through the pages of Kings. As an aside, you'll watch her iron-arm hold on Ahab, her husband.

But your group plans to study something else next? Fine. Take a break from Old Testament history. Study a Gospel, or a letter from Paul, or a topical study. But when you finish, come back. These colorful characters from Jewish history wait to escort you through the story of God's people.

HELPS FOR LEADERS

1 / SOLOMON: PRAYING WITH GOD'S VALUES

1 Kings 3:1–28; 4:20–34

Be sure to read the introductory chapters "I've Joined the Group. Now What?" and "Me, a Leader?" (pp. 9–16) as part of your preparation to lead this study. Point out these sections to your group when they get together. You should summarize the ground rules for them and ask that the group read these chapters carefully during the intervening week.

If you are passing out books for the first time today, your group will not have done the work of "Preparing for Study" (p. 23). Since you will be studying Solomon for three weeks, suggest that they work today's preparation into their next two study preparations.

1. Try to involve each person present with one of these questions.

2. Group members should list the following actions before discussing the second part of the question: made an alliance with Egypt (v. 1), married (v. 1), built palace (v. 1), built temple (v. 1), built wall (v. 1), showed love for the Lord (v. 3), walked according to statutes of David (v. 3), offered sacrifices on the high places (v. 3), offered a thousand burnt offerings at Gibeon (v. 4).

3. Answers should include potential problems for Solomon and for his people.

4. Notice the word *because* in verse 6.

5. Clue words include: servant (vv. 7, 8, 9), little child (v. 7), duties (v. 7), O Lord (v. 7), great people (v. 8), chosen (v. 8), people of yours (v. 9).

9. Keep your prayers brief. Each person may pray more than once if she wants. Allow time for everyone to add something to these sentence prayers.

If your group is meeting for the first time today, you may use considerable time getting acquainted and introducing the study. So if you want to divide the study in half and finish it next week, end today's discussion after question 9.

11. Your group might speculate on the possible outcome if both women had protested the slaughter, if neither had, or if the wrong woman had protested.

12. Pace your study so that one-third of your time remains when you begin question 12.

14. Of course such a group is more likely to see answered prayers. But beyond that, the group will experience the corrective direction of someone who asks for the right things. This person would steer the church or family to godly obedience. (God told Solomon to "walk in my ways and obey my statutes and commands.") Such a person would *know* God. Others would be inspired to experience a similar closeness to Him.

15. Treat this briefly in order to leave time for the final question. In many events, we can't know why God does not answer our prayers in the way we want. But group members should cite some possible problems such as selfish requests, requests contrary to God's law, requests that would unintentionally hurt someone else, requests that would take us in a spiritually unhealthy direction, or requests that simply reflect a lack of foresight.

16. Encourage people to mention specific and concrete actions that would lead in that direction.

2 / SOLOMON: BEARING GOD'S NAME

2 Chronicles 6–7

1. The following phrases should lead to a discussion of God's qualities: *promised, chosen, fulfilled, for my Name, brought, you are not the one.*

2. God's reputation (His name) is interwoven with the temple and all that goes on there. The activities there will reflect on God's name as it is viewed by His own people and also by foreigners.

3. Notice the way he placed himself before God, before the temple, and before the people.

5. Key words on what Solomon asked of God are: mercy (v. 19), hear (vv. 20–21), put your Name there (v. 20), eyes open (v. 20), forgive (v. 21).

But Solomon did not hope to contain God in a temple—or anywhere else (v. 18).

6. The following excerpts should form a basis for discussion:

—continue *wholeheartedly* in your way (v. 14)

—careful *in all they do* to walk before me (v. 16)

—highest heavens cannot contain (v. 18)

—you [God] have kept your promise (v. 15)

Help your group to move from these factual responses drawn from the passage to the more personal: Why might *you need* His forgiveness? Why might *you want* it?

7. Watch your time carefully as you progress through this question. You should have nearly half your time left when you finish question 7. You can save time if you fill in your own chart ahead.

Ask a different person to read each paragraph and quickly note the answers. If the group gets bogged down on a particular paragraph, you can supply the answers from your own chart and go on.

11. You should save enough time to discuss these important questions adequately. Answers should come from all parts of verses 11–22.

12. See verses 19–22.

13. Find four steps for the people and three promises from God in verse 14.

14. Encourage people to speak as personally and specifically as they are able.

3 / SOLOMON: FAITHLESS IN LOVE

1 Kings 11

2. See verse 2.

3. Find several answers in this section.

6. Eliminate this question if time is short.

8. See verses 29–31. Notice that God had already given this message to Solomon (vv. 11–13).

9. a. verse 33

b. verses 35, 37

c. verse 38

d. verses 32, 34, 36, 39

Note: Does ten plus one equal twelve? No, not today, nor by the math in Solomon's time. *New Bible Commentary* suggests that the tribe of Judah eventually absorbed the nearby tribe of Simeon. Therefore Solomon was to lose the northern ten tribes but retain the southern two tribes that eventually became one tribe: Judah.

11. Eliminate or summarize this question if you are running short of time.

14. Idolatry, intermarriage, rebellion, and self-centeredness are some of the sins that might have been root causes of Solomon's spiritual fall.

15. Confession is always hard, so don't expect graphic details. Encourage several people to mention at least one general area in which God is convicting them. Those people who went through the "Preparing for Study" section will already have begun to think about this. Appropriately, they will have gone into more detail in their confession to God.

4 / JEROBOAM/REHOBOAM: CIVIL WAR

1 Kings 12

1. Answers should be detailed and in sequence. Citing verse numbers will help the group stay together. Someone should point out where the two leaders were at the beginning of the chapter, and why.

2. a. In defense of Rehoboam's harsh answer, the proper place for inauguration was Jerusalem. Yet Rehoboam went to Shechem in the North, probably because the people there would not come south to Jerusalem.

Notice Jeroboam's swift return from exile in Egypt—a hostile signal to Rehoboam. Notice also Adoniram, his position, and his death.

b. See verses 10–11, then 14–15, and finally 16.

3. Compare verse 15 with 1 Kings 11:30–31. The events of verses 22–24 prevented unnecessary bloodshed.

6. Find several reasons in verses 26–27.

8. This question assumes some knowledge of the law as given in Exodus and Deuteronomy. Find seven ways in which Jeroboam disobeyed God in these verses.

12. a. Frequency of church attendance is only one area to discuss. Think also about the way you use opportunities for fellowship with other believers. (Do you fight over petty issues when you should be enjoying oneness in Christ?) And what do you actually do and think during worship, public as well as private?

b. Use this question to encourage several group members to plan more effective use of their opportunities to worship.

5 / ASA: SEEKER OF GOD

2 Chronicles 14–16

1. Ask each person to name one action word (verb) in these verses. Then discuss what these actions reveal about Asa's character.

3. a. Your group should find a half-dozen or more implied beliefs. For example, Asa believed that God allows Himself to be found by people—or he would not have commanded his people to "seek the LORD."

b. Answers appear in verses 6, 7, 12, and 14.

5. Ask your group to discuss warnings and blessings separately.

6. a. As you prepare to lead the discussion on this passage, circle in your Bible all the verbs and verb phrases in verses 8–19. This will help you see if your group is being thorough as it discusses this question.

b. Encourage images of everyday life that would reflect this kind of massive reform. (Group members will probably include images of those who reformed willingly as well as those who were forced to reform.)

8. Note on verse 12: The writer does not imply that Asa should not have sought medical care. The criticism is that he asked help *only* from the physicians, and not from the Lord as well.

There is an irony in Asa's disease. Verse 10 shows that Asa put the prophet Hanani in prison. *Old Testament Commentaries* says the Hebrew words indicate Asa inflicted a kind of torture on Hanani that involved the binding of hands and feet in stocks in a twisted position. (Keil and Delitzsch, p. 369). Interesting that Asa should get a disease in his own feet.

9. There is a time discrepancy between the Kings and Chronicles account here. It is probably not important, but if someone points it out, you can give the following information found in Keil and Delitzsch's *Old Testament Commentaries*: Second Chronicles 15:19 and 16:1 speak of the 35th and 36th years of Asa's reign. But 1 Kings 16:8–10 shows that King Baasha of Israel died during the 26th year of Asa's reign. The numbers in Chronicles probably refer to the time that Judah had been an independent nation, therefore the 15th and 16th years of Asa's rule. Since the Hebrew markings for these numbers are similar, the current translation probably resulted from an early copying error.

11. If people have trouble with this question, try smaller questions:

How is this phrase different from, "If you seek Him *you* will find Him?"

What is your part?

What is God's part?

What does the process of seeking and finding involve?

12. Since spiritual development is a life-long process, even those who have known God for a long time must still seek Him in practical ways.

Linger on this question long enough for several people to speak briefly of steps they might take if they wanted to become more diligent in seeking the Lord.

6 / ELIJAH: BUILDING TRUST

1 Kings 16:29–17:24

1. Appropriate phrases include:

—did more evil . . . than any of those before him (v. 30)

—considered it trivial (v. 31)

—married Jezebel (v. 31)

—began to serve Baal and worship him (v. 31)

—set up an altar for Baal (v. 32)

—the temple of Baal that he built (v. 32)

—made an Asherah pole (v. 33)

—did more to provoke the Lord (v. 33)

—at the cost of his firstborn son (v. 34)

—at the cost of his youngest son (v. 34)

2. Encourage several suggestions that reflect an understanding of Israel's deep spiritual depravity.

3. Your group should find 6 or 8 facts in this verse and include some understanding of Elijah's character.

5. b. Go beyond the fact of what was happening, to the truth about God that is represented. For example, the prophecy God gave Elijah proved true, so he could trust what God said to him. God was protecting Elijah from Ahab, so he could know that God valued his life. God was feeding him regularly, so he could know that God would probably meet his needs in the future; God would not forget him.

7. Your group should point out virtually everything Elijah said to the widow, including his approaching a perfect stranger in a deadly drought and asking her to *bring* him a drink. Let your group cite each detail of the conversation.

10. Treat each person separately. See especially verse 24.

11. If you have extra time at this point in your study, also ask, "Why do you think these miracles, so rare in the Old Testament, occur at this time and place?"

12. Look again at each demonstration of supernatural power with this new question in mind.

13, 14. Save ten minutes or more for your group to discuss these questions as specifically and personally as possible.

7 / ELIJAH: MIRROR OF GOD'S POWER

1 Kings 18

2. Your group should point out the following details:
—It was the third year (v. 1).
—They knew they might have to kill the animals (v. 5).
—The king himself was out looking for water to give his stock (v. 6).
—Ahab was looking for Elijah (v. 10).

3. Find answers in verses 4, 13, and 18–20.

5. Group members should point out some of the following details:

—Obadiah was a devout believer (v. 3).

—He hid one hundred prophets of God in spite of the queen's plan to kill them (vv. 4, 13).

—He cared for the prophets with food and water in two separate caves (v. 4).

—He recognized Elijah, God's prophet, as "my lord" (v. 7).

—He acknowledged that the Spirit of the Lord might move Elijah (v. 12).

—He had worshiped the Lord since his youth (v. 12).

—He carried Elijah's message to Ahab even though it might cost his life (vv. 14, 16).

6. Expect some answer from each person present.

10. Your group should come up with a variety of answers. For example: Elijah's life was at stake, so was Obadiah's, and with him the lives of one hundred hidden prophets; further, the authority of the pagan queen Jezebel was on the block, as was the reputation and authority of 450 pagan prophets along with their god Baal; Elijah's reputation as a true prophet was at stake—and along with his reputation, a spiritual trend in Israel would be decided; above all, God's authority and power in the eyes of the people stood to rise or fall. The root question to all of these issues was this: Who is God?

12. Notice the five requests in verses 36–37. The key phrases are "let it be known" and "so these people will know."

14. Note on verse 40: Killing 450 prophets of Baal may seem extreme in our minds. A look at the following passages will help put it into perspective: Deuteronomy 7:1–11; 13:12–18; 1 Kings 18:4.

These pagan priests had led an entire population into pagan idolatry. In addition, they had publicly confronted the living God—and lost. Had they been allowed to remain, the people would have always been subject to their influence.

Time is important at this point in your study. If you are running late, table objections about Elijah killing the prophets, and ask someone to report on these related passages before your next study. Or you can briefly summarize your own findings and then go on to the next question.

15. As your group responds to this question, someone should capture the image of Elijah, robe tucked high, running faster than Ahab's chariot could roll—with the first storm in three years chasing them from behind.

17. Save enough time for several people to speak of personal responses to this question.

8 / ELIJAH: A PROPHET DEPRESSED

1 Kings 19

1. b. Verse 1 shows that Ahab told Jezebel "everything" about these events. Yet her remarks of verse 2 show that she had gained no respect for Elijah or for the power of his God. And she was still calling on the authority of pagan deities.

2. Notice the following places and times (use your maps): Jezreel (18:45); Beersheba (19:4); desert (19:4); Horeb, another name for Sinai (19:8); by this time tomorrow (19:2); one day's journey (19:3); forty days and forty nights (19:8).

5. b. Note: *New Bible Commentary* says the Hebrew words translated "gentle whisper" might more accurately read "the sound of gentle quietness" or even "gentle silence."

6. b. Notice the intervening events between the two conversations. (God revealed His power and Himself.) Yet Elijah continued to despair, even using exactly the same words. Let your group discuss the implications of this.

7. If someone is familiar with the continuing story of Elijah and Elisha, she may point out that Elijah never anointed Hazael and Jehu. Instead, Elisha did (see 2 Kings 8:13 and 9:6). And in fact, he seemed to settle for a mere verbal "anointing" for Hazael. If this becomes a problem, you can suggest that since Elisha was to take over Elijah's position as prophet, he also took over this particular assignment as well.

9. Note: Elijah's words of verse 20, "Go back. What have I done to you?" seem at first confusing. But on second look, we see that Elijah refused to lay down the rules for Elisha's new calling. The call came from God, and both men knew it. Elisha was free to respond to God as he chose.

10. a. Pace your study so that you have thirty minutes left when you begin question 10. Your group should cite the following evidence:

—Elijah ran for his life (v. 3).

—He left his servant at Beersheba (probably because he did not plan to return) (v. 3).

—He prayed that he might die (v. 4).

—He told God, "I have had enough" (v. 4).

—He believed that he was no better than those who had tried and failed before him (v. 4).

—He slept inappropriately (vv. 5–6).

—He recited to God all that had gone wrong (vv. 10, 14).

—He forgot (or didn't mention) the prophets Obadiah had hidden (vv. 10, 14).

—He failed to respond to God's miracles and His personal presence (v. 14).

b. Elijah *talked to God* about his depression. (See verses 4, 10, 14.) And he spoke with a high degree of frankness. He made no attempt to sound holy or falsely cheerful. The self-pity and inaccuracies of his mind are all there.

11. a. Help your group look through the entire chapter again and point out the many ways God gave this kind of personal help.

b. Use your answers to 11a to form more general descriptions of the kind of help God gives His people during times of emotional crisis.

12, 13. Use these questions to move the study from Elijah's life to the lives of the people sitting with you. Help group members respond in a way that is as specific and personal as possible.

BIBLIOGRAPHY

Aharoni, Yohanan, and Michael Avi-Yonah. *The Macmillan Bible Atlas*. New York: Macmillan, 1977.

Alexander, David, and Pat Alexander, eds. *Eerdmans' Handbook to the Bible*. Grand Rapids: Eerdmans, 1973.

Bright, John. *A History of Israel*. 3d ed. Philadelphia: Westminster Press, 1981.

Douglas, J. D., ed. *The New Bible Dictionary*. Grand Rapids: Eerdmans, 1962.

Edersheim, Alfred. *Old Testament Bible History*. Grand Rapids: Eerdmans, 1979.

Guthrie, D., J. A. Motyer, A. M. Stibbs, and D. J. Wiseman. *New Bible Commentary*. Rev. ed. Grand Rapids: Eerdmans, 1970.

Harrison, Roland Kenneth. *A History of Old Testament Times*. London: Marshall, Morgan, and Scott, 1957.

Keil, C. F., and F. Delitzsch. *Old Testament Commentaries*. Grand Rapids: Eerdmans. Reprinted 1980.

Pfeiffer, Charles F. *An Outline of Old Testament History*. Chicago: Moody Press, 1975.

Roberts, David. *Yesterday the Holy Land.* Translated by Ed van der Maas. Grand Rapids: Zondervan, 1982.

Schultz, Samuel J. *The Old Testament Speaks.* New York: Harper & Brothers, 1960.

Tenney, Merrill C., gen. ed. *The Zondervan Pictorial Encyclopedia of the Bible.* Grand Rapids: Zondervan, 1975.

Thiele, Edwin R. *A Chronology of the Hebrew Kings.* Grand Rapids: Zondervan, 1977.

_____. *The Mysterious Numbers of the Hebrew Kings.* Grand Rapids: Eerdmans, 1951.

INDEX